W9-CAO-134

Volume 95 of the Yale Series of Younger Poets

Maurice Manning

Foreword by W. S. Merwin

Yale University Press

New Haven and London

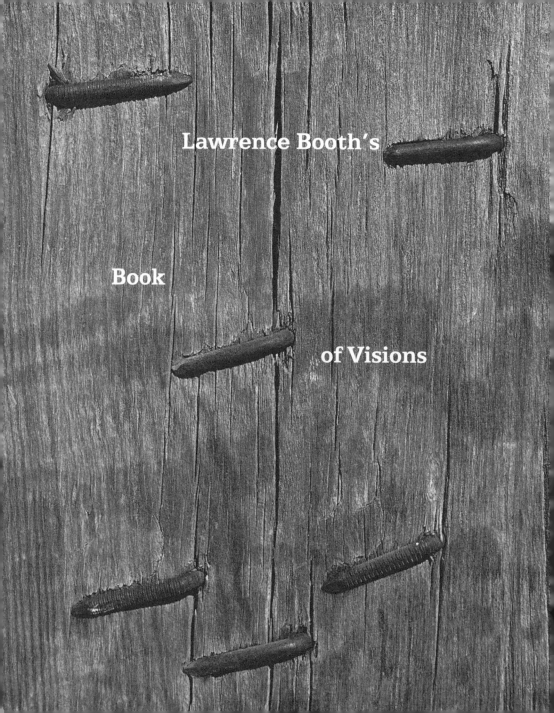

Lawrence Booth's

Book

of Visions

"Ace" and "Reserve" originally appeared in *Green Mountains Review.*
"Analog" originally appeared in *The New Yorker.*
"Eclipse" originally appeared in *Hayden's Ferry Review.*
"Raptor," "Affirmation," and "Canis Apologetica" originally appeared in *The Spoon River Poetry Review.*

Designed by Nancy Ovedovitz and set in Postscript Century Expanded type by The Composing Room of Michigan, Inc. Printed in the United States of America by Vail-Ballou Press, Binghamton, New York.

Library of Congress Cataloging-in-Publication Data
Manning, Maurice, 1966–
Lawrence Booth's book of visions / Maurice Manning.
p. cm. — (Yale series of younger poets ; v. 95)
ISBN 0-300-08996-1 (alk. paper) — ISBN 0-300-08998-8 (pbk. : alk. paper)
I. Title. II. Series.
PS3613.A36 L39 2001
811'.6—dc21 2001000806

A catalogue record for this book is available from the British Library.

The paper in this book meets the guidelines for permanence and durability of the Committee on Production Guidelines for Book Longevity of the Council on Library Resources.

10 9 8 7 6 5 4 3 2 1

This book is dedicated to:

WDC and JYH
HEROES

and

Hank, Hoyt, Cobb, Gangey, The Parson, and Rev. Andre Crabtree
SAINTS OF THE MIDNIGHT CHOIR

Ayre Rectified. With a Digression of the Ayre.

As a long-winged Hawke when hee is first whistled
off the fist, mounts aloft, and for his pleasure
fetcheth many a circuit in the Ayre, still
soaring higher and higher, till hee bee come
to his full pitch; and in the end when the game
is sprung, comes downe amaine, and stoopes upon
a sudden: so will I, having now come at last
into these ample fields of Ayre, wherein
I may freely expatiate and exercise
my selfe, for my recreation a while rove,
wander round about the world, mount aloft
to those aethereall orbes and celestiall
spheres, and so descend to my former
elements againe.

Robert Burton, *The Anatomy of Melancholy*, 1632

Contents

Foreword

The opening lines of *Lawrence Booth's Book of Visions* give us an idea of what to expect from this vivid collection. Authority, daring, a language of color and sure movement, first of all, and a high style of great speed and resource that can range, without apparent change of step, from irony and farce to clear lyrical elegy, from refracted projections of child-talk to direct or costumed maturity.

The individual poems, arranged in three sections, comprise one sequence, with a setting as present and consistent as the sets of a theatrical production, and they bring on a cast of characters who recur in a spectrum of forms and phantoms, luminous shapes altering in the same kaleidoscope. The second poem, in fact, is a "Dramatis Personae" list (which may or may not have been intended to recall the section with the same title at the beginning of James Merrill's "The Book of Ephriam"—Mr. Manning does not make a show of his reading, which must be considerable, and his allusions are cloaked and sometimes mischievous). The catalogue tells us a few crucial things about the personages we are about to meet: oracular details, clues as to how to regard the ballooning figures rather than plain temporal information. For instance, by way of an entire introduction, "*Sissy* is the younger sister hanging by a thread."

It is obvious that this book is original both in the more important primal sense which indicates the source from which it rises, and in the other sense which has become common tender: it is not commonplace, familiar, or of an expected kind. In fact it is wild and strange, and from conception to form, imagery, and vocabulary its author takes enormous risks. Part of the pleasure and excitement of reading it comes from seeing how the poems and the sequence as a whole, step by step, survive, one surprise following another and the parts coming to reflect one another and compose a visionary completeness that is assured, occasionally moving, and soon recognizable without being altogether explicable.

It is, as the title tells us, a book of visions, and the kinds of visions alter as the kaleidoscope turns. They are made up of make-believe, hallucination, memory, fragments of reflected history and legend and fantasized hearsay, dramatized dream, images of wishes and of dread. Most of them rise as fictions of the fictitious Lawrence Booth, known as Law, at different ages of his childhood, adolescence, and young manhood. Some are projections expressed in the caricatured and parodied "End-man Minstrel" language of Law's "pastoral comrade," Black Damon, whose pieces, which have their own recognizable tone and sorrowful dimension, are entitled "Dreadful Chapter One" through "Dreadful Chapter Seven." The visions are not only formalized fantasies, they are consciously theatrical, with Law himself at least partly directing the show, and the theatrical nature of the display allows the shapes and figures their cut-out relief, their layered apparitions and ironies. The visionary cast of the whole work holds one part after another up to the light and shows the planes of time back-lit, one behind another.

A number of interlude pieces occur through the series and step out of the proscenium but not out of the performance. The first, with the theme of loneliness, is "Envoy," a column of want ads, men looking for women. They run from

Man who believes television
is the mouthpiece of the devil,
seeks female with similar views.

Eccentric (?) gentleman (negotiable)-
tinker/farmer searching the heavens
for the true spark of love (breast-size unimportant). Please.

"Proof," another of the interludes, is in the form of a page of a geometry book, with a psychic diagram, columns of *statements* and *reasons* to prove that "The sphere of love exists tangent to the sphere of sin."

A third, "A Condensed History of Beauty," consists of a small chronology, concise but fragmentary glimpses over a period of seventy years, that race past like pages of a rapidly flipped picture book.

The most theatrical of these pieces is a mock Circuit Court document setting forth a Complaint by a local chapter of the Daughters of the Confederacy against Lawrence Booth (age not specified) for entering "the Plaintiff organization's place of meeting," cutting the buttons off the portrait of a Confederate cavalry officer, jumping onto a table and shouting "How now, you secret, black, and midnight hags!"

Besides providing an array of comic perspectives, the out-of-the-frame sections are striking displays of Mr. Manning's appetite for formal variety, one aspect of his rich gift for invention, which charges the current and prosody of his lines, and leaves no two poems quite alike. The personae themselves become multiple characters, or multiple facets of the same characters, or multiple facets of each posing as the whole. They become tantalizing, elusive, images from vaudeville or from fun-house mirrors, while remaining inhabitants of one personal pantheon.

The Missionary Woman, for example, of whom we are warned, in the "Dramatis Personae" that she is

. . . endowed
with certain properties such as transformation

and are left wondering, near the end, about,

> The chance that the Missionary Woman
> is an exquisite work of Booth's imagination.

She arrives on the scene in a brooding soliloquy about guilt and punishment, entitled "Prisoner of Conscience," in which several layers of age and memory seem to be laminated:

> They kicked him out
> for a long list of terrible reasons:
> . . . .
> . . . they confined him to the thirty-seven acres
> and told him his punishment was work
> of the lifelong, back-breaking variety;
> and The Church of the Socially Concerned and Aware
> sent out the Missionary Woman to comfort him with prayer.
> . . . .
> And the Missionary Woman, as it turns out,
> has the finest legs in all of Christendom—
> . . . .
> How strange, his crimes should finally bring him ease;
> his hearth is bright and the praying does not cease.

She becomes, in fantasy or metaphor, a landscape of her own, the river valley running down her sleeping back one of the book's happy explorations.

Two unfailing good spirits accompany Law through all these roles and transformations. One is Red Dog, "the sure-fire antidote to the devil," Law's animal shadow-spirit, another shape-shifter, unquestioning, unpretending, a reliably benign aspect of the world, who sits outside the church and howls during the lack-luster hymns. The other is Law's closest friend, Black Damon,

> . . . a baby-faced black boy
> with big arms . . .

and his own family, troubles, and transfigurations. The grotesque parody of Amos-and-Andy lingo in which Black Damon's "Dreadful Chapters" are couched is startling , offensive, relentless, and the fact that it seems to demand an explanation is, I expect, part of its role in insisting upon the preposterous nature of the radical situation and mores that it caricatures. One cannot help hearing it as an echo of the disturbing ghost of Berryman's Mr. Bones, and a suggestion of the dream-foil way Bones lingers around the warm, affecting, eloquent figure of Damon.

Violence occurs, or threatens to occur, in many of the poems, and the father-figures, especially Law's father, are the source of most of it. Law's father, Mad Daddy "with the shotgun full of history," appears in different pieces as Ole Dreadful Daddy, Ole Black Jack Daddy, Crackshot Daddy, Ninety-Proof Daddy, Heartbreak Daddy, Stumble Down Daddy, Knocked Out Daddy, Bad Gamble Daddy, Stagger Lee Daddy, Real Mad Daddy who shot Red Dog in the hip with buckshot "fer suckin egg an makin ole hen fussy," and Law shouts into a log *"I hate you, Mad Daddy."* In a climactic piece, the next to the last, "A Dream of Ash and Soot," Mad Daddy rides up drenched in kerosene, stands up on his horse and shouts, among other things

> . . . *I love you like*
> *a furnace, son! Heigh-Ho Silver, away!*
> . . . strikes a match on the heel of his boot and turns himself
> into a galloping yellow torch . . .
> . . . and the sun falls down.

And a current of tenderness also runs through the visions, floating the Missionary Woman, Red Dog, Black Damon, and appearing in the landscape of the thirty-seven acres and in the orchard in "Shady Grove"

Booth lazes in the spidery orchard watching
a ladybug navigate the back of his hand
as if the sun-freckled territory seemed familiar—
how she is like a red grain of creeping joy,
and these apple trees like lichen-clad promontories
poking into the middle air, and the shaggy moss
beneath his hand, a shimmering green plain.
Such days come to him like a quivering dove
and he needs no earthly reward for his pains
but this, when his heart becomes a book
of hours and the day becomes its own vessel,
unmoored.

That is, I think, a key passage of an outrageous, lit-up, wide-ranging sequence of poems which in the end prove, indeed, to be facets of one view. The writing's unfaltering audacity is equaled by its artistic control, and the result is an astonishing collection, still more astonishing as a first book; the achievement of a fresh and brilliant talent.
W. S. Merwin

Acknowledgments

This book would not be possible were it not for the kindness of many teachers and friends. First and foremost, I must thank Robin Behn, Thomas Rabbitt, and Bruce Smith, the best mentors I could ever hope to have. I would also like to thank Jean Schwind, Paul Lacey, Ama Ata Aidoo; Bill Campbell, Christopher Nugent, Nikky, Gurney, Jim and Mary Ann, Bobbie and Roger, Kim and Jamie; Matt, Susan, Tim, Alan; Alexi, and D.C. And especially my mother.

I will always be grateful for the generosity and support I received while a student at the University of Alabama at Tuscaloosa. Many thanks, too, to the Fine Arts Work Center in Provincetown for a fellowship which afforded me precious time to work.

Additional thanks to the following journals in which some of these poems were first published: *The Spoon River Poetry Review, Hayden's Ferry Review, Green Mountains Review,* and *The New Yorker.*

ONE

Bellwether

Sheepish as a far off echo, Lawrence Booth wades
into the Great Field and the wide-yawning night,
and swallows down a river of firefly light, which illuminates
the cave in his chest, as if he is one big barn-dance and it is
Saturday night and the kinfolks are coming over with cold
beer and sawdust to make a real party of it. But it turns out
he is the only guest. Words strung together like molecules
flicker in neon along his damp walls, words such as
PsychotropicMetaphysicalLovechildAtOneWithThe-
CreaturesAndTheEarth and L.B.PlusTheM.W.EqualsTrue-
UnfalteringLove and SpinOhUniverseOfHolyRiverlandsSpin—
they whip like horsetails in a kettle waiting to be stirred!
The river forms a deep pool with a carousel whirling
in the middle and none other than Mad Daddy riding
around and around on a flaming horse. The man
operating the machinery calls himself Old Pock-Marked Job!
Dressed up like an Indian—feathers and a dingy buffalo robe—
he shouts to Booth, above the pantings of the calliope, *How!*
this is the wilderness, Kemosabe! which explains the undeserved
suffering and the abandonment and the mocking. Oh, it is
a far-flung shepherd's life! But truth is, friend, this black sea

is an Inscrutable Holy Paradigm, so don't let the strangeness
throw you for a loop! All of which leaves Booth dizzy,
and he whirls through the Great Field with his lighthouse
head, a crazed silhouette hee-hawing and slapping his thighs.

Dramatis Personae

God is the bony man leading the goat-cart
full of garden vegetables, giving them away
to the villagers—cauliflower to the widows,
pole beans to the mischievous boys, cucumbers
to the balding attorneys, potatoes to the gamblers,
turnips to the housewives, middlings to the chickens.

The Missionary Woman is the peek-a-boo
bright star on the western horizon, endowed
with certain properties such as transformation.

Sissy is the younger sister hanging by a thread.

Black Damon is the pastoral comrade.

Red Dog is the sure-fire antidote to the devil.

The *devil* plays himself like a wicked fiddle.

Other characters include various *birds* and *horses*, ancient
stoop-backed *relatives*, some *angels*, a nearly invisible

long-suffering *mother*, select *friends*, a *country* comprising *hills*
and *rivers*, *thirty-seven acres*, the *Indian Tree*, the *Great Field;*
several unnamed *rustics*.

A withering *grandmother* born in a place called Thousandsticks.

Mad Daddy is the man with the shotgun full of history,
the horse and the flame, and the domino shoes.

And *Lawrence Booth*, the bull's-eye boy.

Wave

Wash day, and young Booth is in the yard
weaseled under the whipping sheets like a bug,
lying on his back, bare feet kicking the billows,
right eye winking at the downy clouds, ten dirty
fingers woven in the grass. No one on earth
can see him and no one knows about the tickly
feeling swimming like a fish beneath his breast.
Being the only fluttering boy in spring is all he wants
on such a bright and windy day, while he pretends to hide
from his poor grandmother, the long-widowed sweet one
who lives on top of a mountain, who has the powder box
full of buttons and marbles and the three stray dominoes
with Chinese dragons coiled on the back. The sneaky old
devil has not yet tried to strangle him. Everybody he knows
is a big-boned woman except Mad Daddy. For now, the whispery
world is full of honeybees and clover; it is a very sleepy time
and he has so many sleepy days ahead, plus some terrible ones.

The Hobos

One boy says he is going back home to sleep in a real bed.

The other boy sits down on the dirty ballast and strokes
a matchbox with one finger, flicking a stick of yellow flame
into the weeds. A red dog is crouched beside him with six feet
of knotted clothesline tied around its neck. The night-time smells
like creosote and shirtless boys, mixed with june bugs and grease.

Earlier, they had met a man who was building a fire in a tin can;
he was scratching himself all over and telling a joke about chickens.
The boys got afraid of the laughing man with the pin-head scabs;
they became scared of getting their legs cut off and loneliness.

But still the second boy says: *I swear I'll jump the very next train and you
might never see me again!* The first boy looks back: *Yo pants
is on fire*—and keeps on walking. The first boy is a baby-faced black boy
with big arms. The other boy is skinny as a rail and sings like the rain.

Dreadful Chapter One

Red Dog barkie echo plum back to de house,
Rooster Strut Daddy pissin off de porch,
Mama fevered up in de pregnit bed,
all skeered bad cause Sissy comin soon.
Law out yonder huntin up snakes,
barefoot bustin glass by de rock-skip creek.
Red Doggie run ole possum up a tree;
he barkie echo bounce off de house—
Git home, now, Daddy holler out loud.
Sad sky twisty up all mean an pain,
shudder bunch a angel fixin bring down rain.
Law an Red Doggie fetch em home two thing:
deadeye possum an a copperhead snake;
Hush up, Doggie, Mad Daddy say.

Envoy

Man who believes television
is the mouthpiece of the devil,
seeks female with similar views.

Attention all ladies who like
biscuits: man has gristmill
and two or three acres of wheat.

Are you a woman cast out from society?
Man with thirty-seven acres
and big muscles can provide refuge.

Would like to find sober woman (beer okay),
interested in pick-up trucks, old-time
Gospel music, buffalo trails.

Grown man who likes red dogs
and skipping rocks, hoping against
hope some woman likes same.

Man who lives several hundred
years in the past would like to find
woman zealous for spinning wheels.

Eccentric (?) gentleman (negotiable)-
tinker/farmer searching the heavens
for the true spark of love (breast-size unimportant). Please.

Octagon

A barefoot man with a hoe on a hill;
a woman standing over a salt kettle;
three children swinging from a bull-tongue plow:
mules, a powder horn, a slant-roofed cabin,
two hogs, chains, an anvil, a half-breed dog;
no surveyor in the whole country: free land
homesteaders: a doe hung in the smokehouse,
a river full of fish, stonecutter's tools, sheep
and wheels, wagons, wild fruit, poplar trees reach-
ing Heaven, God unpreached for the moment,
and twenty-six Indians hiding in the woods—
oh, sweet tobacco, cornmeal, archetypal world—
sleep tight. Plus seven shining generations:
a back-talking teenage boy raises his fist
and shouts: *I aint drivin a coal truck, Daddy!*

Ace

Gradeschool days and Booth flies out into the Great Field
to wave at the yellow biplane just in time to catch
the last flap of the pilot's scarf before he roars away.

Booth has flown Mad Daddy's miserable coop, in which
the old preening buzzard was perched in a kitchen chair
crowing about yet another noble tragedy, until his head
flopped back and he passed out with a cackled snort.

The plane tips its wings good-bye; Booth scrambles
to the hay barn and climbs the ladder to the loft
where he has hidden a picture book about the ancient world.

He wants to build a Roman aqueduct from the big hill
straight into the kitchen. He needs roughly
forty-two hundred feet of clay pipe, some pedestals, pillars,
arches, pulleys, ropes, a team of oxen, a furious storm.

Prisoner of Conscience

They kicked him out
for a long list of terrible reasons:
his ways had become old and mighty odd,
his heart had grown dangerously sick with God,
and they claimed his Ole Dreadful Daddy was a skunk.

Of course, there were other, more minor crimes, which,
nonetheless, had very serious implications. For example,
he stopped saying the word *me*,
he refused to watch TV,
and he had the cold audacity
to believe his generation was lost by its own accord.

Consequently, they confined him to the thirty-seven acres
and told him his punishment was work
of the lifelong, back-breaking variety;
and The Church of the Socially Concerned and Aware
sent out the Missionary Woman to comfort him with prayer.

They thought he deserved a life of toil and woe, but to tell the truth,
hard labor and banishment have been kind to Booth.

He does not mind the work or the sweat on his brow
or possessing only beehives and a one-eyed cow.
And the Missionary Woman, as it turns out,
has the finest legs in all of Christendom-
dear Lord, how he loves them!

How strange, his crimes should finally bring him ease;
his hearth is bright and the praying does not cease.

Leather-Stocking

Winter, 1958: Mad Daddy
and his one-eyed brother tramping
through the woods, playing a pair
of great white hunters, hunting God
knows what, anything with fur.
A blizzard comes up, the woods sound
like fatback in a skillet, and the men go
blind. Certain death, except for a light
up the hollow: a fox-faced cabin in the woods.
The brothers take refuge; a mountain
woman feasts them, a mountain man
drinks them. That night: a deep feather bed,
nine quilts, the wind, like sin, shut out.

      Now Booth looks
across the Great Field to a different light,
this time, incandescent. Less wilderness now,
life less fierce, less old. Booth considers
tramping with Black Damon, he considers
nine quilts and winter. He needs a reason
besides hunting, which he cannot abide;
he sees Red Dog like a wolf in the Yukon,
he sees a window covered now with frost.

Dreadful Chapter Two

Why come Mad Daddy make Law play dat game
a tremble-hearted Twenty-One all night
an leave de kitchen such a fearsome sight,
Law's Mama say it oughta be a shame?
An why come Law git stuck wit such a name
dat leave he alway cipher wrong from right—
so much he git a tooth-clench mood to fight?
He wonner if de Lord could deal de same
sad hand to any other boy. But least
Law got Red Doggie piller-hip to lay
he head, instead de kitchen flo. Dat leave
Ole Black Jack Daddy head slump back like a beast:
he chair a cage, he wrist gin de ashtray,
de Ace a Spade asneakin out he sleeve.

Proof

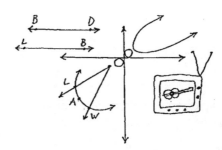

Theorem: If a boy's memory is locked onto an illuminated grid, then he will spend his life looking for the skeleton key in vain.

Prove: The existence of Hell.

Statements	Reasons
1. The slope of Mad Daddy's money clip is zero.	1. Given
2. The array of Mad Daddy's tactics includes forcing the whole family to holler whenever the man with the Red, White, and Blue guitar appears on the black and white plane.	2. The intersection of 90° rage and the ellipse of Saturday night forms the line known as *Hee Haw on Channel 17*.
3. The hypotenuse of the Great Field is the direct path Booth takes from the back porch to the Indian Tree.	3. Boyhood = secret trails, hideouts, trapdoors, plastic telescopes.

4. The volume of mercy poured on Booth directly corresponds to the graph of his need.

4. Red Dog's Parabola

5. The circumference of the frying pan is half the length of the trail of blood leaking out of Mad Daddy's head.

5. If the angle of incidence crosses the plane of reflection, the result will be the arc called *LAW*.

6. The line of schoolchildren who laugh at Booth's shoes and high-water blue jeans is parallel to the line laid down by Black Damon.

6. One Blood Brother $\geq$ The Other

7. The sphere of love exists tangent to the sphere of sin.

7. ∞

Therefore: the Devil whistles Dixie from the hole beneath his tail.

Shady Grove

Booth lazes in the spidery orchard watching
a ladybug navigate the back of his hand
as if the sun-freckled territory seems familiar—
how she is like a red grain of creeping joy,
and these apple trees like lichen-clad promontories
poking into the middle air, and the shaggy moss
beneath his head, a shimmering green plain.
Such days come to him like a quivering dove
and he needs no earthly reward for his pains
but this, when his heart becomes a book
of hours and the day becomes its own vessel,
unmoored. Booth wants to tell the pagans
to smash their plastic gods. Have them roll up
their sleeves beneath an apple tree and watch
the spotted angels festoon their heathen wrists.

A Prayer Against Forgetting Boys

The boy with the burned up face.
The boy walking across the railroad bridge.
The boy who saw everything.
The boy who ran to the hills and hid in a cave.
The boy racking balls at the pool hall and sweeping up ashes.
The boy from his own country.
The boy painting a fence.
The boy with the brains God gave a goose.
The boy who took thirteen rabies shots in the belly.
The boy with the horse somebody shot.
The boy with pneumonia and salve on his chest, long ago in a dim log house.
The shoeshine boy popping a rag.
The boy with one eye.
The boy with a memory shaped like a tree.
The boy who threw rocks at a train.
The boy who kept dreaming of flames.
The boy digging a trench.
The boy who never flinched.
The boy climbing a silo to send out a plea.
The boy with his hand on the neck of a snake.
The boy on a wagon covered with hay.

The boy swooping across the plain of time.
The boy who learned how to be a boy
thanks to an infinite dog.

Seventeen

When two boys are unloading box
cars and pulling pallet jacks around
or when they are stacking haybales
on wagons or when they are cutting
firewood against an overbearing wind
or when they are trying to get old cars
to start: they must talk loudly about girls.
So it was with Booth and Black Damon—
one with a gas can at the carburetor,
the other revving the unbridled engine.
The news from Black Damon: a skinny
girl had taken her finger to the down of his
raven lip and said she liked his nearness.
Then there was severe nearness between
them which caused Black Damon to laugh
in the re-telling of it, because he was
shocked by the sight of hips and something
else, which he gave an unrepeatable name.
The news from Booth: no, he did not spill
his seed on the belly of the magic cheerleader,
though he wanted to.

It was her skirt
waving like a white surrender flag. It was
Booth sinking through his shoes, running
to the Indian Tree, where he carved
a six-letter word of protest.
Black Damon
turned grim and said if it would make things
any better, he had a cousin Booth could get
in another town, though she was kind of heavy.
Booth put the gas can down, his face a sheet;
Black Damon let the big car die.

Progress Report

Dear Mr. and Mrs. Booth,

Lawrence seems to have a hard time paying attention,
even when we are discussing subjects that interest the other
children, such as fur-trapping or pioneers or Conestoga
wagons. He spends a lot of time looking at the trees outside,
or drawing miniature pictures in his themebook; pictures,
for example, of a little boy holding a frying pan and a man
lying on the ground with crosses over his eyes and blood
pouring out of his head. There is a grinning angel presiding
over the scene. Another picture shows a boy with a shovel
in a grassy field. He has scraped away some grass
and has drawn something in the ground that looks like
a tiny constellation. There are several pictures of horses
with wings, flying above what appear to be flames, as well as
drawings of a dog with large teeth, carrying the boy on its back.
Frankly, the other children are not sure what to make of Lawrence's
colorful imagination. He often mentions having a fort in an Indian
Tree. And the other day, he terrified a little girl, passing her a note,
asking her to *please be* [his] *forever sacred heart*, which sent the child
home in tears. Later, he told the class he was a direct descendant

of John Wilkes Booth, explaining the assassin was *only one
of the devils God has let loose in the world.* And today, during a film-
strip about The Oregon Trail, Lawrence crept up to the blackboard
and drew a frightening picture of a skunk clutching a pair of dice;
what could be the head and source of your son's distemper?

Ontology

Booth's description of the sea: a floating body
in the outline of Mad Daddy and a boy
in a rowboat hugging the shore, one oar,
like a bad leg, shorter than the other.

Booth's conception of science: a game of lines and numbers
in which negatives count for more than they should.

Booth's notion of modern love: clear-cutting,
reserved for heartless lumberjacks.

At the scene of the Crucifixion, Booth sees:
a bystander peeling back the flesh from a wound,
revealing a tiny television in the Body.
On the screen, a black boy groans, tied
to a tree, and another boy fumbles
with a pocketknife, trying
to cut the black boy free.

Pontiac

The black car planted under two twisted locust trees,
one hubcap left: the profile of a proud Indian
bowed down: three feathers, chrome, a bullet hole.
A boy laid across the front seat; it is Booth, roughly
twelve years old, dreaming away in the musty rat's nest.
Glove box yawning open, a dusty tongue covered
with a couple of wheatback pennies, a church-key,
Mad Daddy's dogtags, a crushed pack of cigarettes.
The boy perceives the voiceless moment: he hears
a grim man charging two mules locked in a yoke
to drag the carcass to the edge of the field. A pocket
radio singing in the boy's right ear, antenna sticking
out the broken window, left arm screwed around
the steering wheel. The radio tuned to the Old-Time A.M.
Gospel Show, Sister Elsie Marie Gearhardt playing guitar
and chromatic harmonica. A man in the background
slapping his boot on a wooden box. The mid-1970s
to a boy in a junked car, with a radio. He feels six inches
under a shiny pool of wind-blown water, like a breeze
tied down. He closes his eyes, lays eleven miles of steel rail
in his head, scatters buffalo to freedom, and paints a thundering
picture of the Glory Train, a trail of soot falling back to the earth.

Dreadful Chapter Three

Law's Pore Mama bury four boar hog toothey in de yard
say her broken down famly need ever stroke a luck dey can git—
keep corn nubbin stretchin an Ramble Off Daddy home a lil bit;
she plum tired a livin dis cheatin shoestring life so hard.
Law been growin like a weed an pore Sissy shore need
a Easter dress ana whole mess a other perty girl thing—
an Crackshot Daddy he blow a bull's-eye through a smoke ring,
say he gonna shoot de Easter Bunny an chop off he lucky feet.
But Law git a bad notion a where de money went,
so he git hisself a big-time shoeshine job at de barber shop
an buy he Mama bobby pin an bring sweet Sissy sody pop;
he spit-shine bankerman shoe, two pair fer twenty-five red cent.
Den Law take dem hog toothey to de wood an burn em up;
a hard-workin man wit a fear a God dont need no luck.

Strait

Black Damon piled on a stoneheap shaking
his head no, and Booth drunk as a lord shouting
out what they load rick by rick onto straight
trucks: hen fruit, three-roll barking dog, hoglegs,
poke bales, manhole covers, Just-For-Girls coffee
in number ten cans, salt blocks—and railroad
coal dust like unleavened bread on their tongues.
Booth falls down in the field and says he feels
like he is drowning in his father's river.
He wants to lay a laurel on Black Damon's
head. He waves to the genius of the shore
and wonders which women fall for working men.
He wants love to be something more than just
another venerable disease. He waves
again to Black Damon mounted high, and sinks.

Quantum Cowboy

Stellar keen on animal husbandry, Booth scoops and gathers sweet grain
for the nodding creatures, scattering finger-long mice from the feedroom:
shoo now, mousie, and the mice swim away to the shadows
like three gray fish in a pool. Buckets clatter and the sky flashes
as if the angels are playing with the lightswitch again, and Booth hovers
through the burned out orchard, where a procession of broken spider webs
wraps around him like rough banners from a gang of old world clans
intent on forging a pact against enclosures and the dread feudal lord.
He looks into the flickering heavens and wonders why the brilliant scientists
with their satellites and laserbeams ever bother sending radio waves
into outer space, given the consternation over the vague components of light.
But Hopalong Booth has hardly any use for such swirling tangents of speculation:
it is the end of a long day and Booth feels mighty lucky, for the old house looks like
a dancehall gleaming in a windswept frontier town—he has a silver dollar in his boot
and the Missionary Woman is the prettiest barmaid in the whole lawless territory;
he sashays like a high-roller through the swinging doors, tips his hat,
pulls out his magic deck, and asks his sassy lady to cut the cards.

Beck

Black Damon's nicknames for Booth:

1. Eddie Earl
2. Thirty-Seven
3. Griggs
4. Bumpo

Booth's nicknames for Black Damon:

1. Crispus Attucks
2. Hawthorne
3. Chandler
4. Dred

Analog

The collision of three deer and a flock of martins;
fur and feathers, two kinds of flight, two exceeding
champions of grace, flutter and flash; both possess
necessary tails, black eyes: they love their young
to pieces, peck and lick, their own kind of kisses.
Special features: iridescence and musk, split lips
and beak, gizzard and rumination, distinguishing tracks.

Beautiful bug-eaters, traipsers through the grass
and sky! Keep bobbing your heads, nip and tuck,
across the river between you! Forget the dull limits
of classification. Consider the twin trunks of the poplar tree
pointing pell mell, divining the Great Field. Fear neither
live-birth nor hatching!
                          Oh, revelation only ever comes
at sudden crossings—Booth's heart hops like a happy frog.

Siding

Zero hour and the train stiffens, frozen in its tracks,
waiting for the weary switchman, accustomed to
literal midnight, to swing his bright lantern: it is a scene
in which a treacherous, yellow-eyed serpent is paralyzed
by its own beautiful hiss. The world wears a gray cloak;
the yawning union man floats out of the fogbank glowing.

A lantern dangles from one invisible hand, the other
cradles the silhouette of a sledgehammer. He waves
the light, as if he is saying: okay, I threw the switch
and the rails slid over; go drop off the three cars stuffed
with lumber—poor boys from town will unload the mess
tomorrow. The steel-muscle shrinks and tightens.

Two miles away, Booth and the Missionary Woman
are snuggled up like a pair of thieves in a barrel,
his working-man's hands around her.

Soon Iron-Horse Booth drags the steaming
Missionary Woman piggy-back. His legs are twin
burnished pistons, she is the delicious

coal-tender car spilling soot down his neck,
the Red Dog plays the faithful caboose;
everything could be right on time.

·

A Condensed History of Beauty

1907:   A man digs a deepwell on a hilltop, harnessing
gravity, resulting in free indoor plumbing.

1926:   A man and a woman sit in a country parlor by a fire;
she reads *Sonnets From the Portuguese* out loud; he falls asleep.

1937:   A boy rides a chestnut gelding twenty-six miles
to town and twenty-six miles back without bouncing once.

1939:   A boy cracks sixty-three hickory nuts with a hammer;
a woman proceeds to bake a legendary cake.

1944:   A boy takes a shotgun to a freightyard and blasts
lead patterns on the sides of boxcars.

1945:   A man picks up a coal bucket and his heart explodes; two mules
drag his casket up a hill; the preacher recites "The Crossing of the Bar."

1951:   A young man writes his mother from Korea:
It has been turrble colt in this Godforsaken two bit place, ha!

1965:   A gambler wins thirty-seven rocky acres and a rough-hewn house
in a card game; he hangs a sign by the road: *Trespassers Will Be Shot in
the Knee.*

1972:   A boy climbs a tree with a slingshot in his teeth; he has a powder horn
full of pea gravel and shoots at a washtub; it sounds like a church bell.

1973:   A boy listens to a transistor radio while lying in a burned out car;
that night, he tells his sister: *Today I heard you singing from a little
silver box!*

1976:   Two boys take the foot-brake off of a bicycle. One boy sits
on the handlebars. The peddling boy says: *Let's close our eyes.*

TWO

Pegasus

An exceptional dream, a long moment
of half-sleep, the century slowly grinding
to a halt: he feels like a royal Arabian horse
with black eyes is pouncing—two hooves—
on his chest, then, the desire for featherweightiness
or a ribcage made of tempered steel, plus the cucumber
smell of a snake in a ditch; everything very ticklish now
and the horse is thirsty, hopping like a primitive
firewalker, white mane turned to leaping flames.
So Booth leads him to the river, water running
over blue rocks, a mouth exhaling, water weeds
waving on a rocky tongue and Booth sweeps his hand
like a salesman around the riverland scene: *Looky!*—
(two honey locust logs, a toy tractor, scrap iron scatterings,
hemlock boughs, a spooky house, a sunken barn;
the bleak hand of a man, the hem of a woman's
yellow dress, a boy's scabby knee, a girlchild's hair
blown back by the breath of God) and, finally,
the horse stops jumping. Booth's lungs uncollapse.
He thought he was drowning, but then he surfaced.

Antimatter

The echo of a wretched day hops around in Booth's poor heart
like a frog with a lame back leg and leaves him hugging
his coldly sculpted torso, so he seems all shoulders and breast.
The bright thoughts fall, canceled out by the dull memory
of calamity and the spreading indifference of the world. When it is
no particular day, no single sorrow at the root, how can Booth
still stand for love? He cannot believe in a callously random universe,
the spark that ignited the big bang, the wild coagulation of proteins
longing for webbed feet in a puddle. Now it is autumn-time,
after the harvest, and Booth feels left out. He stirs up a cauldron
of dead leaves and sets it on fire. A wave of blackbirds flaps across
the sky, a battle flag flecked with powder burns. The Great Field
looks like a leper colony and Booth stands frozen at the edge,
a weathered statue before an overgrown garden, a disfigured shade.

Dreadful Chapter Four

Silly Sissy pull de laig off nine brown cricket
an drop em half daid in Mama's black skillet;
she fill de house wit fried up cricket stink,
Mama scream loud an pour de whole mess down de sink.
She wonner if dat gal ever could keep clean
an wash Sissy lil hand in stingin kerosene.
Ninety-Proof Daddy laugh till he red eye had enough,
den he smoke out back wit he sleeve roll up.

But Law dont see a single funny thing—
worry dat gal got somethin wrong in her brain:
he sound like a holy ghost way he beller an sing
an walk two mile, bust a rock gin a train.
Law heap a full-growed weight on his lil heart
evertime he love me tender famly try to fall apart.

Allegory

Late one night when the first hint of spring was singing through the air,
Booth had a strange dream, in which he turned himself into a tree:
he went to the woods, kicked up the leaves and gathered a handful
of sundry seeds, mixed them in a bucket of rain water,
then poured the potion into his brain, and lay down in the Great Field
until he sprang up out of the dew and grew into an enormous
hybrid, a wild, deciduous thing bearing nuts and berries and delicious
fruits that hatched from his blossoms. And he fed his people well;
they crushed him in vats and made wine, they took his sap and made
a sweetening agent, and his oil became a source of light. The villagers
called him The Glorious Swooping Tree of Booth and Sunday afternoons
they had picnics in his shade and their children tied swings to his boughs.
Songbirds built nests in his branches and he hollowed out a room
in his trunk where the Missionary Woman lived very happily; the rain
and the sky were his friends and the dirt around him was his heritage
and eventually a deep river cut through the plains and curled up beside him.
All was well, until an unexplainable grave bitterness overtook a handful of villagers
and they cut him down and shredded his skin into paper to print their ridiculous
political tracts, and the garish ones fashioned his breastbone into dashboards
for their luxury automobiles, and the warmongers carved his thighs into propellers
for their fighter planes, and the counterculturalists tried to smoke his roots,

and the grim-faced television crew captured the last sad bird flying away (Back
to you,
oh, Hard-Grimacing Dan!). The only part of him that remained was the hollow,
which the Missionary Woman decided to fill with provisions and launch into
the river;
she raised a sail on his bony mast and said, *Oh, you, and your cantankerous visions
of peace*, then patted his gunwales lovingly and they sailed for another land.
The Red Dog was perched in the bow, a peerless good-luck maidenhead with teeth.

Affirmation

Hayseed Booth's hard-worn hands: the Missionary Woman's
glorious knees and long shanks: the Red Dog sunk in the grass
like a bug: the Great Field: one brightly blooming
seventeen-acre picnic.
The groundhog: mad-dashing
from one subterranean love-den to another, hustling
corncobs and walnuts. Forty-three screaming birds of varied colors:
flitting and jigging in the greenery.
Gloom and snakes:
completely subtracted from the bucolic scene.
Booth's mouth: a chamber full of lavender kisses and one passionate
diatribe about the merits of fishing and rivers in the homeland
leap-frogging over exuberant blue rocks. Irony: living simultaneously
in the low age of blame and the age of guiltless indulgence,
plus the boastful age of snickering. The serious question:
Who is responsible for this terrible patch of violets?

Future Booth

Fifty-nine will carry him twenty-five years
into the spanking new millennium, an age of such
promise it cannot be real. By then, the great granddaddy
of all atom-smashers will have frittered away its squalid half-life
and be confined to a flaccid existence as a mere exhibit
in the National Museum of Twentieth-Century Hoaxes and Frauds,
surrounded by gawking china-doll statues
of famous American statesmen and television pioneers.
Booth and the freewill Missionary Woman
and their curly blue butterfly children
and the thirty-seven acres will be
the only world left that still spins.

And he will swing his golden pocketful of history from a chain,
leaping late into the new century
with a flaming strut, like the sun
bursting into a hollow, cutting away the darkness,
calling to the steadfast morning glories;
and he will shout with the voice of a mountain:
Oh, Love has never been free! Come,
stumble down from your double-helix stupor,
oh, my super-conducted people!

Raptor

The mother lets loose a lead sigh, *Lord Ham*
Ercy is it ever hot in that kitchen! and the family
bows to bless the food and the gentle hands
that prepared it. Everything could suddenly
turn harmonious, but Booth cracks one eyelid
and sneaks a peek at Mad Daddy, staring at a wild-
life watercolor of a hawk perched on a fencepost,
pecking through a fresh kill. Three feathered
strains of beauty fly circles in the boy's heart.
One, the image of the hawk itself, a red-tailed
parcel of perfect pitch. Two, the smell
of the father pretending to be
a steel-eyed radius. Three, a terrible
Presence flapping around the room.

Dreadful Chapter Five

Heartbreak Daddy take dat road-whore woman,
like to kill Law's Pore Mama, she cry her blue eye out,
sit nine long day in a sad kitchen wit bad bafrobe shiver
an her skinny leg stuff down in de ole houseshoe she wear;
Stumble Down Daddy finely come home wit he cigarette lip
an wonner why in hail scramble egg again, an he shout,
say Law's Shaky Mama oughta calm her silly self down;
den Law take fryin panhannel an turn cold as lead
an raise a cast iron knot on top a Mad Daddy's head.
Knocked Out Daddy lay on de flo real long while,
Mama hug up Law an say, My brave lil chile;
den Law run to de bafroom see he muscle in de mirror,
an make a jackknife tattoo of de Ole Ragged Cross:
Bad Gamble Daddy better learn who's boss.

Seven Chimeras

The way Booth makes an orchid:
combine one bluebird with nine fencerow
pokeberries; crush together and hang
thirty yards away in half-light.

The way Booth makes a story:
never know the beginning;
uncover pages hidden under river
rocks. The rocks contain a mineral
called unforgottenite. Watch out for snakes.

The way Booth makes a nightmare:
pretend there is a jug of Mad Daddy's
ninety-proof novocaine sitting on the picnic
table. Swallow it. Get in the car and drive
until both eyes burn out of the rear-view mirror.

The way Booth makes a love story:
same as a regular story, except
under one rock is a trapdoor that leads
to a room full of bellybuttons;
each must be pushed, one is a landmine.

The way Booth makes hope:
thirty-seven acres, Black Damon,
Red Dog. Construct a pillar of fire
in the Great Field and let it become
unquenchable.

The way Booth ends the Jack-in-the-Box charade:
shoot the weasel in the neck
and toss it to the buzzards.

The way Booth thinks of salvation:
God holding a broken abacus,
colored beads falling away.

Act V, scene iv

The smell of rain swarms the air;
the moon, circumscribed like
a pebble dropped in a pool, pours
down on Booth, hip-deep and ablaze
in the Great Field. He cloaks himself
in the pheromone of harvest-time.
The last hay stuffed in the barn;
everything looks like a pumpkin,
even the clouds are coming in swollen.
What keeps this field from becoming
a seventeen-acre magic carpet and floating
Booth away to his tent at the oasis?
Where is his ruby-tressed harem? Was one
plump belly-dancer too much to ask?
A breast, a breast! My kingdom for a breast!
slips from his lips in a whisper. Earlier,
he had opened one of his favorite books,
A Cavalcade of the World's Literary Treasures,
volume 2, and a silverfish crawled like a kiss
out of the Editor's Preface to "Selections
from Shakespeare"—and Booth was jealous.

Now he raises a limestone fist to blind
the moon and wheels around like a stranded
king, horseless, vaingloriously hoping
the God of Rain still approves of him,
or else will drown his savage lust like a bug.

Calumet

A boy, a baking powder can containing
seven red feathers, two buffalo nickels:
his mother saved the can for him because
it had an Indian head on the side,
plus a peace pipe. The boy took the nickels
from his grandmother's dressing table:
her room smelled like powder. He found the feathers
spread out on a rock by the creek, coonprints
in the mud beside it. Mad Daddy called
Black Damon's people coons, but Black Damon's
feet made different tracks. Black Damon gave Booth
an amber flint and said, pretend it stops
your chest from feeling shattered.
                                        That night
after Mad Daddy passed out in the yard, Booth
took the can and shook it in his father's sunken face,
said Black Damon could not kill a redbird;
then rubbed the flint like ash against his breast
and laid a feather on his father's lips.

Complaint

Daughters of the Confederacy,   )   Civil Case #___2 7 2000___

John Hunt Morgan Chapter,   )

         PLAINTIFF   )

)

V.   )

)

Lawrence Booth,   )

         DEFENDANT

COMPLAINT

COMES NOW the Plaintiff, Daughters of the Confederacy, John Hunt Morgan Chapter, and says unto the Court as follows:

1. On or about the day of September 4, the Defendant, Lawrence Booth, intentionally, maliciously, and wantonly entered the Plaintiff organization's place of meeting and irreparably damaged property owned by the Plaintiff organization; specifically, the Defendant, Lawrence Booth, took a pocketknife and cut the buttons from the uniform in a portrait of the Plaintiff organization's namesake, who was a highly decorated Confederate Cavalry Officer.

2. Following the desecration of the Plaintiff organization's property, the Defendant, Lawrence Booth, leapt upon a table and shouted, "How now, you secret, black, and midnight hags!," thus causing members of the Plaintiff organization to fear imminent and grievous harm to their person.

COUNT ONE

3. As a result of the above mentioned acts, the Defendant, Lawrence Booth has committed a Trespass to Chattels.

COUNT TWO

4. As a result of the above mentioned acts, the Defendant, Lawrence Booth, is guilty of the Tort of Outrage.

Dreadful Chapter Six

De shivery blackberry winter day Law turn ten,
Stagger Lee Daddy come home singin drunk again,
say he got somethin extry special fer a boy name Law:
give him a ten-cent box a crackerjack—dat's all;
Mama holler in de kitchen, come see what she make,
an light nine shinin candle on de ole birthday cake.
But Law run off yonder to de Injun Camp an cry,
his lil heart so fretful sick he start thinkin sewercide;
he fetch a capgun to de sinkhole an kneel dere on de ground,
den pull de silver trigger an like de echo way it sound.
But Red Doggie whine an git his doggie self afraid,
den lick Law's teary face an save dat terrble day.
Red Doggie nuzzle Law an wag he tail all curl:
Law love he Doggie friend de best in dis wide world.

Like a Tree

The boy stood in the shadows with a makeshift
travois rig, hitched it to his Red Dog's back and looked
out at the far woods like a trapper. He would cross
the river and the railroad tracks and keep on going.
A list of his supplies: a hatchet, some fishing line
wrapped onto a spool, a pair of hooks;
the makings of a teepee, sixteen biscuits, a canteen,
and his great-grandmother's hope-chest quilt.
He was tired of algebra and inclined planes—he cried
out against The Very Heavy Vector which creates
the terrible pattern of falling apart; he was determined
to look for The Mighty Force Which Pushes Back:
he might have to steal a poor man's coal, he might
need to sneak into a widow's kitchen for a cup of coffee;
there could be long nights of keeping watch,
no telling how long he would be gone; so he made
a secret note— 👁 + M 🍃 + ing 🐿, Law—
and put it on his mother's pillow; he had his scoutknife and
a book—*The Ways of the Indians*, copyright 1923. He sent forth
a four-letter word to curse the threat of winter and skunks,
winked at his daddy's dark horse, tapped the dog
with a willow switch, spit through his teeth, and left.

THREE

Exodusman

Nine bluejays scatter like leaves blown down the road
as if one mad gust had knocked the last stubborn notion
from the crooked apple tree and left it naked.
He does not like the bluejays, for they are ungentle
and make poor friends, but he lets them alone,
especially now in the fall when no nesting is done,
and the winter will be evenly hard to everyone.

He has a good woman and a limp
and he goes on with his lonesome work,
despite his hobbling ways and his tendency
to mix prayers and curses together.

Two days ago,
wearing a canvas tarp like a robe,
he ventured out in the rain;
just in case, he had a crooked stick in one hand,
but the blind cow followed him
straight to the barn.

Missive

One morning, Booth was playing the game that he could snap and flash
into town with a five-gallon can, fetch three dollars' worth of kerosene,
and sneak back to home-base before the slumbering Missionary Woman
    woke up.
But he saw two skinny men at the gas station, leaning against an old car
full of turnip greens and fishing poles. One man's legs were so cruelly twisted,
it looked as though God had put them on backwards; nonetheless, the man
    was laughing,
slapping dust from his trousers, as if he had just heard a real good joke.
Booth made a hasty retreat and soon found himself sitting
in the Great Field like an Indian, pretending all he had ever seen
laid out before him was plains and prairie dogs playing in the sun,
and he wished all he had to consider was painting savage flames on his pony.
But the dreadful scene with the twisted legs and greens was too much
    for Booth,
so he went inside, took a magnifying glass, and began closely examining
the sleepy-time Missionary Woman's bare back. Much to his dismay,
a little white feather had sprouted from her shoulder, and her spine
curved away like a lazy river, and a tiny civilization had sprung up at the head
of a valley, dispersing its shining culture through all the land. There was even
a viable class of merchants and artisans, and a miniature skin-tone cathedral

complete with mosaic depictions of the Passion and a couple of bald-headed monks

painstakingly copying sacred texts from papyrus onto vellum; and a boy, living in a hut by the river, was working quietly in the light of an oil lamp, preparing a message to leave in his bottle: *No matter what the city-states and haughty empires say, love is a funny little circle. Spread the word!*

Canis Apologetica

An old man with a shiny red face says
that he likes to feed coyotes anti-freeze,
which they love the way bears love honey.
They creep up at night to a bucket in the pasture
and drink. The man laughs and his eyes
wink together—life is like a heavy machine
the world keeps trusting until it finally breaks
down; death is the grim repairman who says
it cannot be fixed, despite the fact that yesterday
it was working fine. The same man smells like
barbershop tonic. He loves his stooping wife.
They have been married forty-odd years.
He pats his hand on the back of Booth's neck.
Now Booth smells clean and all concerned parties
smile for the reassuring, old-fashioned community
moment. Booth is carrying two quivering sacks
in his hands: one is full of retribution, the other,
brotherly love. He feels as though he lives in a howling swivel chair
with a three hundred sixty degree view of the wilderness:
he has an image of God: a barrel-chested shape with a razor.

Dreadful Chapter Seven

Real Mad Daddy shot pore Red Doggie hipbone
fer suckin egg an makin ole hen fussy
den he smak lil Law in he sassy head an say,
Next time, Red Doggie gonna lie like a rug
all still, I kill him deader an four o'clock,
and Law run way off down to de Injun Tree
where he keep he secret camp
an holler up a log, *I hate you, Mad Daddy,*
an he cipher out a plan to git Mad Daddy back
fer leavin his red frien half cripple up.
Seem Ole Daddy tear apart ever thing Law love.
Buckshot Doggie he limp aroun four day,
fergit he pain den lick Grinnin Daddy hand all sweaty,
but dat Law: he wonner how Ole Daddy like a limp.

The Bootleggers

Booth and Black Damon sitting on a bench
in a run-down house full of card players
and whiskey; high school twisted into one un-
bearable filibuster of tangents and Magna Cartas.
Black Damon's Outlaw Daddy, called Burrhead,
bald stealer of women, rustler of hogs, dogs,
and white-faced cattle, fashions a terrible plan:
employ the boys—easy green money, no police.

Eighty-six miles round-trip in a '72 Caprice
the color of death, Black Damon white-knuckled;
the dirt road crosses a shallow creek, the car drags
bottom on the sinking way back: seven hundred
dollars' worth of shimmering half-pints. Booth:
blacked out in the backseat, already unforgetting.

Feud

The men Mad Daddy shot did not
have time to blink. The lint
flew off their coats, backlit
by the sinking sun. The men
had names no one can remember.
One man evened the score;
the second man evened it more.
When they fell in the dust,
Booth was just a germ
in Mad Daddy's brain, a dream
in his blood, and the law against
vengeance had not been invented.

Schism

The last lackluster hymn snapped the final
straw for Booth, twelve years old and full
of vinegar—the first straw being the cruel
admonition: he should not bring that dog
to church and wave at the wild red beast
through the window, so that it starts to howl
during the altar call—which seemed silly since
everybody else was filled with the spirit
of wailing and the dog was just chiming
in, sorry for his sin (piercing Mad Daddy's
tender flesh on a whim!)—Booth believed
all God's creatures were bound for heaven.
Undaunted, Booth returned the next week
with his dog and a shivering feedsack, leapt
before the nodding crowd and said: *Anybody
here wanna see this Red Dog wrassle a snake?*

Look Away

The white boys who ran over Black Damon
were rich, their car a gaudy symbol, their
fathers upstanding—Black Damon not:
his empty shoes squatted like a pair
of toads in the gravel. Blue-summer
dusk: Booth saw Black Damon
flying through the air, a burst
of black feathers; he saw
the white boys' shining faces,
silver dollars dancing
across their eyes.
He saw

**Black
Damon's
bare feet**

winking in
the grass; he put
his hand to the hot
county road; he smelled
sin hanging in the air; he felt
the fog lick his neck. He picked up
Black Damon's bloodless shoes and set
them on his shoulders; he felt the heavens
shudder from the scene; he was sure his old
kentucky home had become a dream against the law;
he was full of vows and tears and wanted hard
to
lash
out.

Airlift, 1971

A kindergarten boy draws a fat crayon
picture on yellow construction paper
to summarize one of his recent fireball dreams:
Mad Daddy stuffed in a submarine, sinking
in a whiskey sea; two blue fish upside-down
with Xs on their eyes. Overhead, a boy flies
by in a plane. The Red Dog is the grim
bombs-away figure aiming for Mad Daddy's
bug-eyed periscope. A rope drags tightly
behind the plane, pulling the Indian Tree
and the boy's spotted rocking horse: mother
and girlchild snug in the saddle. A lime-green
sun hangs in the corner with a smile; three
block letters scrawled on the fuselage: LAW.

Braves

Black Damon sits sick from smoking grapevines,
the campfire pops sparks into the starless sky.
Booth propped against a stump, the puptent
sags in the shadows. Booth opens his blood-brother
knife; the eye of night-time looks down on the boys,
tight in the clutches of the thirty-seven acres.
Red Dog stares at their glistening palms.

The thunder cuts into the midnight and Black
Damon grows scared. The tent leaks like a sieve,
Red Dog shivers and whines, and Booth decides
the devil is beating his wife again. The boys
wake up in a puddle; young Booth's hand
has left a purple smear on Black Damon's back.

Eclipse

Yellow moonlight glows in Red Dog's eyes
until Booth steps before the dog's gaze
and his eyes go dark. Booth, head bowed
in the Great Field, beseeches the heavens
to remove the stone of death from his chest;
not his death but Black Damon's, who lies
in a pale bed, swollen with melancholy
knots tangled up inside him. Black Damon
looks like an old television set turned off,
one vacuum tube holding its breath to keep
a dot of light glowing in the midnight room.
Booth falls to his knees; his shadow runs
back to him, and Red Dog's eyes blaze up
again. Black Damon's death would sorely
diminish Booth. Spare him. Cover him.
Swipe Your hand across this cold moon.
Raise him up. May this not happen now,
may this low beast have no reason to howl.

Raid

For three nights now Booth has been going
over a seasoned moment, composing
the list of things that cannot be killed.
The covert scene in dispute: a boy looking
at a VFW calendar on the wall: "In Flanders
Field Where Poppies Grow." It is 1973,
a spring day. On TV, uniformed and
gunless gray men float off a dark plane.
One man looks into the air as if
he is planning to hold his breath before
swimming some river he sees. The boy
imagines the river and hopes the man's
lungs are strong. The boy wants the man
to take off his medals before he hits
the water. The man's hair waves back
like a field whipped in the breeze, like
smoke from a stick pulled out of a fire.
Mad Daddy's hair is wild. He has just one
dirty word and a preposition to describe
the present matter. For days, the boy
keeps wondering if the man made it across

and Mad Daddy swears the sun did not go
down on the man in the water. The boy
wants to know who is Charlie, and his father
finally says, nobody you want to know.
Mad Daddy could be gentle even though
he could spit his words like gravel from a tire.
Booth concludes the boy looked at the calendar
to see if history had a face he would remember.
So far, there is only one thing that cannot be killed: rivers.

Relief

Inkwell in one hand, with one black finger,
Booth is turning the Missionary Woman
into a topographic map, tracing
each contour, indicating which way water
would run if a river divided her
landscape. The black ink is indelible:
if some futurist discovered the parchment,
he would know how Booth marked the burial
mounds and plainly see the cartographer's
smudged fingerprint just above the place where
two terrains must have discovered confluence—
a draw and a hill—because it looks like
ink got spilled and the trembling map maker
tried to cover it up, as if it were
a secret place, although the legend says
nothing about it, not even a hint.

Reserve

1. A cousin's black Cutlass, fifteen years old
and rusted out, and his prom date's get-up—
godawful—a choking pack of cigarettes, and Booth's
feet, clad in Mad Daddy's sure-fire domino shoes.

2. The uncertainty of Salvation, the smothering
number of angels floating through Booth's head,
and Mad Daddy's persistent accounts of old-time
hellishness, in addition to the wealth of Booth's
first-hand knowledge, then the forget-me-not
time Booth laid his neck on the railroad track
and came up with a streak of black grease on his throat.

3. The chance that the Missionary Woman
is an exquisite work of Booth's imagination.

These are things Booth keeps tucked under his hat.

Dovetail

Two thousand winsome years wave
bye-bye in his brain like a field
of English oats, leaving him smack
in the middle of the following fishhook
scene: his own image on the back porch
splitting hairs with a jackknife, Red Dog
hopping through the Great Field like a smart-
aleck seahorse, three indigo birds crossing
the blistered sky. Booth jumps to his feet
and shouts: *I have a severe triangular*
praise, but I am not saying what it is!
Then he backs down: never, never, never
in a hundred sorrow-clad years—Oh,
the vulnerable Self, the Self in collusion
with the ransacked natural world! Oh,
the archetypal knick-knack paddywhack
dolorous process of becoming! Why
are certain flowers designed to catch the dew?—
Rooster-faced, a two-word phrase to describe
the humanity sunk in Booth's heart. *Golgotha*,
like a terrible language, messed up, inscrutable.

Probably, the heaviest adverb of all. *Gravity,*
a familiar over and over feeling. One more
thing: *Rose,* past tense of the infinitive (irregular).

A Dream of Ash and Soot

Wednesday dusk and Mad Daddy, drenched head
to toe in kerosene, canters up, jerks the reins
and stands high on the speckled rump of his horse,
then winks at trembling Booth, eighteen
in the woodlot and tough as a ten-penny nail:
>   *Yeehaw!! to the dread rattling thunder*
>   *I have given fire!—It shore has been some*
>   *rough magic, aint it boy? But now I break*
>   *my staff and drown my book. Forsooth, you have*
>   *your Daddy's country blood! I love you like*
>   *a furnace, son! Heigh-Ho Silver, away!*

Then Mad Daddy snickers, strikes a match
on the heel of his boot and turns himself
into a galloping yellow torch. And his flames
reach to Heaven, and a cloud swirls
through the Great Field, and the sun falls down.

Pilgrims

Here come the crows!
with their fat gleaming breasts,
their leathery feet, their nutcracker beaks,
their perilous eyes and tribal squawks,
their famous longevity, and all
the other noble crow traditions!
They look like low shadows from an odyssey,
strutting along the hem of the Great Field,
like high-born magi shaking off the desert,
or perhaps weary cartographers, or messengers,
or brave pioneers. And what good fortune!—
Booth can give them sanctuary—he has a near
plenitude, with the thirty-seven acres, the Great Field,
the tip-topping trees, the blithe creek,
and he is half-lathered from wildly galloping
around to make them welcome, kowtowing
and paving their way with a trail of cracked corn
and sunflower seed. Oh, send word to the tiny wrens,
the speckled finches, the hoot owls, and all the other
immigrants: the black darlings of the field and sky,
the raven-tressed wayfarers, are at last arrived!